AF316697

Embracing the Sunset Years and Looking Ahead

Embracing the Sunset Years and Looking Ahead

DAVID H. ROSEN

Foreword by Nick Denning

RESOURCE *Publications* · Eugene, Oregon

EMBRACING THE SUNSET YEARS AND LOOKING AHEAD

Resource Publications
An Imprint of Wipf and Stock Publishers
199 W. 8th Ave., Suite 3
Eugene, OR 97401

www.wipfandstock.com

PAPERBACK ISBN: 979-8-3852-0565-3
HARDCOVER ISBN: 979-8-3852-0566-0
EBOOK ISBN: 979-8-3852-0567-7

VERSION NUMBER 112023

Also by David H. Rosen, MD

Educational & Scholarly

Evolution of the Psyche with Michael C. Luebbert

Medicine as a human experience with David Reiser

The Tao of Elvis

The Tao of Jung: The Way of Integrity

Transforming Depression: Healing the Soul through Creativity

Patient-Centered Medicine: A Human Experience with Uyen Hoang

Soul Circles: Mandalas and Meaning with Jeremy Jensen

Lesbianism: A Study of Female Sexuality
with a Father-Daughter Dialogue with Rachel Rosen

Valor to Live: Beyond Despair

Synchronicity and Individuation: A Primer of Jung's
Analytical Psychology

Collections of Little Poems and Haiku

Clouds and More Clouds

Every Day is a Good Day

The Healing Spirit of Haiku with Joel Weishaus

In Search of the Hidden Pond

Living with Evergreens

Look Closely

Spelunking Through Life

Torii Haiku: Profane to a Sacred Life

Warming to Gold

White Rose, Red Rose with Johnny Baranski

Night Owl Haiku (with Robert Epstein)
Roses: Collection of Little Poems

Novella & Personal Story

Opal Whiteley's Beginning & Hoops and Hoopla

Memoir

Lost in the Long White Cloud: Finding My Way Back Home
Torn Asunder: Putting Back the Pieces
Finding Love and Life: Healing the Soul

Children's Books

Henry's Tower
Kindergarten Symphony: An ABC Book
Samantha the Sleuth & Zack's Hard Lesson
Time, Love and Licorice: A Healing Coloring Story Book

Cookbook

The Alchemy of Cooking: Recipes with a Jungian Twist

I dedicate this to my grandfathers: Karl Middendorf and Abraham Rosen, who were both called Pop. This tradition continues as my dear granddaughter Ember calls me Pop.

The best and most beautiful things in the world cannot be seen or even touched. They must be felt with the heart.

—HELEN KELLER

Contents

Acknowledgments | xi
Foreword by Nick Denning | xiii
Preface | xv

Chapter One: Meeting Angel Number One | 1

Chapter Two: Dreaming the Future | 8

Chapter Three: The Art of Suffering | 13

Chapter Four: Living in and with Nature | 19

Chapter Five: Every Day Is A Good Day | 25

Chapter Six: Meeting a Goddess in a Far-Off Land | 29

Chapter Seven: Blueberries and Poetry | 32

Chapter Eight: Personal History, Spirituality and Analysis | 37

Chapter Nine: Reflecting On How Fortunate I Am | 46

Chapter Ten: Physician, Heal Thyself | 56

Afterword | 60

Acknowledgments

The first person I want to acknowledge and thank is Nick Denning who wrote the Foreword and typed the manuscript. At the time, he was a philosophy graduate student working on his master's degree concerning feminism and environmental philosophy; Next he will work on his Ph.D. in Philosophy. I also thank James Miller Jr., Rene Good & Tina Smith for their additional assistance. And, of course, I acknowledge the constant and invaluable support of my extraordinary wife, Lanara. Plus, I want to emphasize the contribution made by Willa, our adopted rescue dog.

Foreword

Every day, like every life, has a sunset. But what does it mean to embrace something like that: a color on the horizon that we can't seem to hold? Sunsets often evoke a sadness within us that is difficult to name. Words like 'end,' 'finality,' and 'darkness' may come to mind, and the emotions that those words carry. In this book, David Rosen's fourth memoir, I find someone who has found a way to name not only that difficult sadness, but the deep shades of joy that accompany them. David considers himself fortunate. Perhaps surprisingly, he does not find this energetic will "despite" his illness, Multiple Sclerosis, nor does he find it "despite" his age. Dave does not antagonize these parts of himself. Instead, he sees MS as "My Savior" and "My Setback." It is a barrier that keeps him from hiking the forest-hills around his home, and at the same time a passage "into wholeness."

David's fourth memoir, *Embracing the Sunset Years and Looking Ahead*, details his life between the ages of 75 and 78. While the style of this book is linear, that line is loose, knotted to its own past and history. In his present David sees reflections of the past, and his narrative carries that past into the present. David also thinks about the future, looking ahead towards what he calls "Mount Eighty" and towards what this world might be like after he passes. Tying together each of David's stories is a feeling of love for the people he has met, and an optimism about what the world can give us. This is true, even when he brings harsh realities to light: meeting the grandchildren of those bombed in Hiroshima and interviewing those who have jumped off the Golden Gate Bridge (and survived).

I met David through the unlikely circumstance of a job application. A professor of mine (I'm a graduate student in philosophy) advertised David's request to hire a private typist. I was curious. After driving to David's house deep in the hills of Southern Eugene — deer, even bears, abound — I was struck to find such amicable company. David is old, but clearly wise beyond his years. His accumulation of stories and poems don't exist only in print but speak through his contented and conscientious living.

Like the view of a sunset, you will find in this memoir colors and emotions that contrast, though always with the impression that whether something is ending or beginning, we are capable of finding beauty and meaning.

Nick Denning
Eugene, Oregon

Preface

This volume is my 4th memoir. It deals with only three years: 2020 to 2023, which allows for more commentary about the character and meaning of these years. The Talmud says that immortality requires three things: Have a child (*I have three*); plant a tree (*I have planted many*); and write a book (*I've written thirty*). As we know, most writing is autobiographical, so reading my numerous volumes would tell, altogether, the story of my life and its adventures. Readers have gone with me to Greece, France, Denmark, England, Scotland, Spain, Brazil, Peru, Japan, Russia, China, South Africa, and Switzerland. And they have even ventured to specific places, such as the Shetland Islands in the U.K., Graceland in Memphis, Tennessee U.S.A., Daitoku-ji Temple in Kyoto, Japan, and Machu Picchu in Peru, South America.

Unlike most memoirs, this one covers a very specific three-year period (75–78). In numerology 75 signifies hope, wise reflection, and a connection between the conscious and subconscious. Dreams link the two. What is amazing is that 78 represents achievement, balance, and a process towards wholeness (like Jung's individuation). It can be interpreted in two ways: the first is that I have accomplished things in the past that work their way into this memoir and the second is poetry, because through it a certain balance can be achieved. So, this book opens and closes with angels. I hope and pray that this is a sign that I'll get into heaven with angels next to me.

Angel is like the Arabic word "Hafaza" which means take care, guard, protect and defend. Hafaza is very similar to a guardian angel. All these characteristics are meaningful and natural parts of this memoir. Hence, in other words, I have been looked after and guided by these celestial beings. Plato maintained that the beginning is the most important part of the work, and using that philosophical view, I begin with my journal of 2020. Fortunately, since I was eighteen, I have kept a daily record of dreams and events recorded in a religious manner. The actual journals are or will be preserved in my archives at Texas A & M University [TAMU].

Memoir requires self-reflection, self-examination, which fortunately can lead to self-healing. It underscores what Mary Tilton said in "Artist's Prayer."

"May my work reflect the light and the shadows that are my
 being,
May I have clarity.
May I know when and where to begin and
When and how to stop.
May I always have the strength to ask the hard questions, to
 peer deeply
Into the dark pools,
The patience to wait for sediment to clear."

David H. Rosen, M.D.
Eugene, Oregon

Chapter One

Meeting Angel Number One

Be content with what you have, rejoice in the way things are. When you realize there is nothing lacking, the whole world belongs to you. Turning 75 in 2020 brought me into direct contact with an angel, which means messenger. So, what was the message? It was that I would live a long time. I am conscious of the fact that in Japan (which I have visited three times and once with my three daughters: Sarah, Laura & Rachel) 88 is a meaningful number. It could represent my age of 88 at the end of this wonderous life. We know that the length of one's life is unknown. However, it has a lot to do with what Hafaza is. For instance, what we do and eat, as well as who we relate to and what we believe in, has a lot to do with our time on this earth. On my birthday, (February 25, 2020, I turned seventy-five), which is ten years older than my father's age when he died. But, my mother, Barbara, made it to 93. However, let's return to that magical year when I turned seventy-five.

This year, 2020, started with the usual Happy New Year. On the first day, I was recovering from New Year's Eve. On the second of January, I slept too late, as I didn't set the alarm! I had been having trouble sleeping, mainly due to the pain in my neck, left leg and lower back. The very best analgesic for my pain was and is being with Lanara. I feel no pain or very little, when I'm with her. That's what love can do for you!

Embracing the Sunset Years and Looking Ahead

White roses
in memory of
a lost loved one

This poem was about Atova, who was a wise older woman that Lanara and I both cared about, and who loved us both. Lanara told her that we would plant white roses in her memory, which we did. They were her favorite. The symbolic meaning of the white rose is peace.

Frustrated about oversleeping, I calmed down and noted my dream: 'Going to prison but lost.' I was in prison for succeeding, I wondered why doing well was a crime. Perhaps succeeding just like failing isolates us, in some odd way. I felt like I was imprisoned, having MS. I felt and feel trapped. But Lanara revealed that I am not alone, and that I am not dying. Her view helped me to accept my chronic neurological condition and that my mind was good and creative. However, I was upset that I was ill and that there was no cure for MS. I have found an escape from prison, though: writing.

One of the things I was distressed about was that I did not travel like I used to. I managed to go back to Texas A&M University [TAMU] regularly, until I retired in 2011. However, I continued to host the Fay Lectures in Analytical Psychology through 2014 and edit the Fay Books through 2017. Editing the 20 volumes and writing the forewords for each of these books was a creative process that I thoroughly enjoyed, and which helped me learn so much and respond to each vital topic in an innovative way. Carolyn Grant Fay endowed these efforts and she also helped establish The Jung Educational Center in Houston, Texas. On one of those trips, I met a man who said that he had recently built a guest cottage. And I thought, that's just what we ought to have built, where we live. I say that because both Lanara and I like to be alone, especially when meditating and creating.

Now, back to 2020 and this memoir.

On Sunday January 5th Lanara and I went out for pizza at La Perla. We recalled that we had been there long ago, when our eight-year-old grandson, Ben, visited. Again, it was fun and delicious. Wow, in 2020 Ben started going to the University of Texas in San Antonio. As we know, time flies when we are having fun and improving our minds.

Our days are quiet, which I am sure is true for other elderly folks. However, I feel privileged to be with Lanara, who was a cook for orphans, when I met her in New Zealand. She is altruistic and loves gardening. We have amazing gardens with veggies and flowers...even four kinds of roses. Every day she makes wonderful meals. I'll give you an example: she makes unique pizza[1] for us and she adds all kinds of items, like Italian sausage, tomato, cucumber and broccoli (which she grows) – and then we have a salad using lettuce and cherry tomatoes that she cultivates. Nevertheless, I love to take Lanara out to dinner at Beppe and Gianni's Trattoria. At home, Lanara has even made her own sausage, which is a real treat. And she liked to roast Provence Chicken in a special Italian clay pot with spices and vegetables, including potatoes. For dessert, we are fortunate to have Coconut Bliss (a local coconut-milk based frozen dessert) – now changed to Cosmic Bliss. Another thing that I am fond of are Halva bars, which are made entirely from sesame seeds and coconut syrup. They are delicious. For all those interested in the spelling of "dessert" (vs. "desert"), according to Nick's third-grade teacher, Ms. Pawlowski, one spells "dessert" using the 's' twice, because they should always want more dessert. Whereas "desert" gets one 's,' because one is out in sand and often with no dessert.

In my other memoirs it becomes obvious that I like to read various books, like John Muir's writings – which is not the usual for psychiatrists or psychologists. Because of him I felt inspired to make a retreat center for creative quietude modeled after his work. Related to his ideas, we would like to leave our home and property as the 'Rosen Retreat Center' with 30 acres and three trails. There would be a caretaker in residence, while a painter or writer could apply for a place to birth their artistic products (paintings or books). Previous recipients of this position would nominate others

---

1. There is a long history of unique pizzas, going back to Pompeii in 79 A.D.

to stay in this special place. Incidentally, this was the way I selected future Fay lecturers and book authors, using recommendations from previous participants.

Let's return to the use of our home as a creative center. With two bedrooms and accompanying bathrooms, on opposite sides of the house, a caretaker could stay in one place, while the visiting artist or writer would be in the other section of the residence. There is a large common living room with a deck overlooking the forested acres and a Franklin stove in the living area. There are lovely views, and the deck is perfect for sitting outside to work or have a meal, and for viewing the spectacular sunrises and sunsets. The selected individuals would be cautioned about poison oak, bears, and cougars, which also share this environment.

Given my condition, at some point the individual becomes unable to walk on his or her own. For years, as the MS progressed, I used a cane to move about, but since then I have relied on two walkers (one for the inside and another for the outside). On this day I went out with my blue "Evolution" walker on the path that we constructed that goes around a pond that's in front of our house. Lanara's gardens sleep during the winter but wake up in the spring and summer and are still lovely in autumn. Lanara has grown many flowers and trees surrounding this pond, along with a large garden area to the west of our home. Long ago, we installed a path that circles around the pond and through the gate into the garden. This way I had a regular place to walk. Having the foresight to have put that path in was a blessing, since it has become very handy.

On June 29 of 2020, I dreamt that I was funded by a French grant to study ancient dead in Turkey. In an odd way that is what I am doing writing memoir, as that genre is all about what has happened in the past. Although not related to Turkey through my personal history, I can relate to half of my identity being tied to where my father's family came from: Romania. Abraham, my paternal grandfather, was given a bicycle by the King of Romania, Carol the First, and told: "Ride this to America." He must have known that America was spoken about as a land of freedom. Abraham's father, Sandor, was a pastry chef for the king, which may have motivated the King's kindness to Abraham. While King Carol upheld laws that restricted important elements of Jewish life (like obtaining citizenship), this story shows that he, or someone on his staff, may have had a soft part in their hearts for Jews. Later Abraham was able to bring his father to America, where he was a pastry chef in a Catskill's resort in New York.

There is a significant cultural, historical, and geographical relationship between Romania and Turkey. On my mother's side is German and English ancestry. Both countries had much to do with Turkey's role in the two World Wars. For example, in the first World War Turkey joined with the Central Powers (Germany, Bulgaria, and Austro-Hungary) to combat the English. The country's neutrality in World War II minimized the German influence on Arabic nations to Turkey's South. All this to say that my dream of studying the dead ancients of Turkey makes some sense when looking at my ancestry – sort of.

Again, I celebrated July 4th in 2020 with "Bangs and Roman Candles." Even though Lanara does not like fireworks, she has enjoyed the lights of roman candles.

The day after the Fourth of July, I was at home, which is conducive to meditation and miracles. A couple of days later, I wondered how did the SB (Supreme Being) know to send Alex to us, and why? Alex is like the son, Luke, that we never had. I have always wanted to have an heir like him. Hence, I am thankful that we have, not only Alex, but Nick, as well as two grandsons: Aiden and Ben. Shortly thereafter, Sarah John, a physical therapist that helped me a lot, taught me exercises that were valuable. We walked outside, and she told me to keep walking.

Next Alex came and we went to take our taxes to our accountant. As we know, the two things that are sure to happen to us are taxes and death – of course there's birth too, and rebirth.

In the night, Lanara woke up worried about Covid-19, the state of our health, and the world. I understood completely, and I chose like her to not think about it and pray for the best outcome. Nevertheless, we got the necessary vaccines. I continued to do analytic therapy, which allows for thorough and deep personal work.

During the weekend I sat outside a lot, writing and enjoying the sun. It's lovely weather around 70 degrees, and no rain. We thought that it would rain a lot in Oregon, but so far this has not been so. Climate change has been making a difference.

I sent out a proposed flyer for my 22 books with Wipf and Stock Publishers (this number has since increased). On Tuesday, July 14th, Alex came, as we would traditionally dine out. I did this in appreciation for all he does for us. We went to Chef's Kitchen and ordered their salmon dinner (salmon, potatoes, and vegetables). At Harvest Episcopal Church, we ate and walked. This was a sustaining practice, coupling the spiritual with the gourmet.

Seventy-five
happily married, but
falling apart

This little poem, written in 2020, documents how I felt at that time. The tension of opposites is vital to both Taoism and Jung's psychology, which is probably why I am fond of both. There is a difference between the feeling of "falling apart" and the optimistic view that every day is a good day, of which I am fond. It sounds like a paradox, but that's where meaning is found. Accepting one's illness can lead to positivity, and that's a better road to go down than the other one.

Three books were published in 2020: "*Soul Circles: Mandalas and Meaning*" with Jeremy Jensen (an artist who originally came to see me looking to become a Jungian analyst), and who drew the mandalas in this book. a second memoir "*Torn Asunder: Putting Back the Pieces*," which covers ages 30–60, and a third volume "*Every Day is a Good Day*," which is a children's book.

I dreamed of a couple in therapy, which Lanara and I did in Texas, a preventative step for living fully in Oregon. It rains a lot here, which we expected it to do, as we both like that gentle sound – but then it became colder with snow. However, this area does not get as much snow as the Cascades. As I mentioned, we like to go out to eat at unique restaurants. Occasionally we go to a Thai restaurant – there's a good one called Ta Ra Rin. We would get Tom kha, tempeh, and a spicy green papaya salad.

MS plagues me. An example, is my feeling terrible because I can't put my robe on. Yikes! Occasionally I would go to dinner with Erik Verdouw, a former physical therapist, and we became friends. I also discovered that one treatment recommended for MS was massage – and I can vouch for the fact that this is true.

Around this time, I treated Alex and Krissy, Alex's fiancé, to dinner at Sushi Domo [a Japanese restaurant] as a holiday gift. At this time, I was also working on a new book, "The Tao of Dave: A Collection of Aphorisms,", which eventually became *"Soul to Soul: Aphorisms for Life,"* which was published in 2021. It was a practice of mine to go to a teahouse called J-Tea from time to time. Here, I would meet Steve Shankman or Mark Unno. They are both professors at the University of Oregon. The first specializes in Comparative Literature between Early China and Ancient Greece, and the second in East Asian Studies. They, like myself, have written many articles and books. Finding it difficult to leave academia, I currently am an Affiliate Professor in Psychiatry at Oregon Health and Science University [OHSU].

Chapter Two

Dreaming the Future

I dreamed that Lanara was upset with me because I had organized a boat-trip to Mexico without talking to her. My associations to the dream were to be sure to ask your spouse about everything. And, I have always liked to travel, something which is not possible now. And what this dream really meant was that my anima [Jung's word for the feminine side of a man's psyche] needs to be with me, which is the secret of a man's creative writing.

My next dream was about a visit with Kobe Bryant, I met with him, his wife, and their daughter in their home. We had supper but I got sleepy and had to leave. To do this would be impossible now because he sadly, and recently, died in that helicopter crash. However, this dream also touched on my love of basketball. This passion is described in the second part of a small book called "*Opal Whiteley's Beginning & Hoops and Hoopla*" released in 2018. The latter part describes Coach Shep and Shimer's College basketball team, which I was the center for and our national record of 37 straight losses in 1962–1963. Later this record was broken by Towson College with 41 straight losses in 2011–2012. By the way, Shep was an alcoholic. On the way to games he would have the bus driver stop at a tavern and have a drink and he would allow us to have a soda or even a beer, telling the bar tender that it would help us decrease our pre-game tension. Some players would refuse it, but at times I accepted, thinking, "What the hell, we're such a great team!"

One time we were playing in Chicago, at a small institution and at halftime we were behind by just a few points. Shep said that he would not even drink or smoke during halftime, because "We could win this game!" Another loss! In another contest we were playing Eureka College in Illinois (Ronald Reagan was the most well-known alumnus). I was shocked when I first entered the auditorium. There were bleachers full of fans, cheerleaders, and a pre-game warm up. These were new experiences for us. During the warmup, there was a player on our team whose height barely reached 5 feet. He slipped on his own practice pants. Another player was called for double dribbling immediately upon the start of the game. A different player, an older Italian fellow, had a noticeable beer belly. Few of the team members had ever played basketball in high school. You can imagine what those fans thought when they saw us warming up for the big game. But fortunately, I could give them a tiny thrill. I was known for being someone who could dunk a ball. Even in high school, folks said I could jump "real high." Despite my scoring 23 points in one game, we never won a single contest.

One of the guards on our team said: "We should really have some plays, Shep." And, he said, "Okay." I'll give you a play, which he called "Rosie." And, when asked to explain, he said: "Which ever guard has the ball, and if Rosen is open, pass to him." Any team who had any sense would realize "Hey, they only have one play!" Clearly, it wasn't a secret, but that was characteristic of Shep, to have no plays or eventually only one. To his credit, at times we came close to the other team's score, but we lost every game. At one point, this losing streak of 37 straight losses in 1962–1963 had its own Wikipedia page., but that changed in 2011–2012 when Towson College had 41 straight losses.

Another thing I like to do is painting. And the painting below is an example. There's a honey suckle bush near the pond in front of our house, which I include below.

The pond fills when God sheds tears.

Empty pond
where is the rain to
help with the pain?

On November 8th 2020 Joe Biden and Kamala Harris were on TV. Having different leadership in our country, and anticipating the new programs to come, was refreshing after the problematic Trump presidency. The insurrection, an aftershock of Trump's regime, that occurred on January 6th 2021 was organized by President Trump and his associates (who are now being indited, and hopefully convicted). That was a somber day, particularly because we had never witnessed such an incident [storming of the Capitol] in our country. I am thankful for Biden because his and Trump's administrations was the opposite. Whereas Trump did away with a lot of federal programs, Biden reestablished them. And Biden tried to get preschools paid for by the government (which is all of us). Who wouldn't want preschools? However, this was not done, as it was blocked in Congress by the Republican majority.

In November, as I was walking outside around the pond, I felt whole. I noticed a blue heron and wrote:

A great blue heron

rises up

and lands peacefully

The wonderful blue heron left quickly, upon realizing that there are no fish in this pond!
Outside, eating lunch on the deck with Lanara, a cool breeze rose up and our sleeping dog
Willa, slept. Looking out from our deck, we saw a mock orange, peach tree and an artichoke plant with artichokes ready to pick.

Lanara left me a note on Christmas Eve: "David, a faithful friend, is a strong protection. A person who has found one, has found a treasure. A faithful friend is beyond price, and its value cannot be weighed. A faithful friend is a life-giving medicine." What a lovely holiday gift.

During this time, I worked on *Soul to Soul: Aphorisms for Life*, a book which was released in 2021. This book was an important text and I felt good about it being published. I often refer to it. This book was reviewed by Jacob D. Salzer in *Frogpond*, the main American journal of haiku. Among other things, Salzer kindly wrote: "I especially appreciated Rosen's words, "*The feminine mat-ters,*" when he wrote: "The tie between the feminine and these important aspects of human life are very ancient, and are found in many traditions, which refer to the earth as our mother. The importance of the feminine is brought to life in Jungian psychol-ogy, which calls us to discover our anima – the feminine aspect of our psyche."

My experience as a medical doctor also informs some of these aphorisms. In "Physician Heal Thyself," I cite Hippocrates, who said "It is more important to know what sort of person has a disease than to know what sort of disease a person has." Of course, both are important, It is vital to go back to ancient Greece and to the roots of our medical tradition, in order to see what has been forgotten. As I have written in *Soul to Soul:* "Modern medicine of-ten focuses on the disease only and fails to take a holistic perspec-tive of the person. But it is critical for the physician and patient to heed the ancient healing advice about being a healer. This lesson is quite special to me. For being a doctor myself, upon discovering that I had multiple sclerosis, I struggled to come to terms with my own diagnosis. My neurologist who noticed my startled re-action said: "This is not a death sentence…there are treatments." But, that did not diminish the shock nor have the medications and treatments brought me back to health. However, MS has taught me much, and prompted me to begin thinking holistically: chang-ing my eating habits and lifestyle choices. I have learned to call on creative insights and doing things that I've never done before. In this way I heal parts of myself that doctors alone cannot impact. The following poem, which is also the name of the next chapter, expresses the need for each of us to bow our heads and endure suf-fering as part of life even as we strive to heal ourselves and others.

The Tao of Dave
slow and steady
around the pond

Chapter Three

The Art of Suffering

This chapter, "The Art of Suffering," starts with this poem of the same title:

I bow my head in shame
for all the killings of self and other.

I bow my head in sorrow
for inner and outer wars.

I bow my head in suffering
for all the tragedy that exists.

I bow my head in synchronicity
for we are all the same.

I bow my head in surrender
as it leads to acceptance.

I bow my head in prayer
since it is all we have.

I bow my head in love
as that is all we need.

I bow my head in ecstasy
to balance all the agony.

Embracing the Sunset Years and Looking Ahead

I bow my head in peace
and everlasting gratitude.[1]

Where we live is in the country, south of Eugene, Oregon. This Pawnee prayer captures the spirit of our place:

Earth our mother, breathe and waken,
leaves are stirring
all things moving
new day coming
life renewing[2]

Lanara's gardens are a great way of witnessing the world's renewal. She's also made bird baths around the property which provide water for not only birds, but other animals, who come to drink out of a large water tank. Also, beyond the windows are these lovely tall oak trees. Whereas in Texas, the oak trees were shorter and stretched out horizontally.

1. Rosen, David H. *Soul to Soul: Aphorisms for Life*: "Physician Heal Thyself & The Art of Suffering," Resource Publications, 2021, pp. 8–9.

2. "Earth Our Mother." *O, Sweet Nature*, accessed July 19, 2023.

This painting with a red torii gate allows one to get to the garden and pond in front of our house, as well as to enjoy the tall trees. One can see how the water flows out from the pond after its been filled. When sitting on the bench I can see the overflow come down to the right of where I'm sitting, making a small stream. The oval frame often symbolizes nature's own feminine essence, life is renewed, days yield to night, and all things continue in their quiet movement. This is the essence of Mother Earth. I love the bench next to the pond because the stillness finds me. This is also the way that I met Lanara, on the South Island of New Zealand in Allendale Reserve (park), on a bench.

Related to what I have mentioned before: Marrying a great cook was a stroke of genius. Dear Lanara cooking for orphans impressed me, as it was altruistic and kind. Eating well is part of our being together. For example, one recent night we had ham and a lovely salad, which contained home-grown lettuce. Also, her potatoes were added and yes, she grew those, too. In sum, I feel blessed.

Now, back to 2020. It's important to say that most days are quiet. Both Lanara and I love to read. During this time, I read John Muir's writings, which relate to our plan to save our property as a natural place where folks can visit and animals can live freely without fear of being hunted and killed. We have seen bears, including a mother and cubs. Later we saw them climbing trees.

The year ended on December 31, 2020, after a peaceful Christmas and a fun New Year's Eve. This celebration began with a dinner at Sushi Domo [a Japanese restaurant]. The reason we chose this spot was because I used to go to dinner there with Alex every Tuesday night. The party continued afterwards when I went back home to watch the ball drop. Truth be told, I am a night person. Whereas Lanara went to bed early, which she usually does. However, I like New Year's Eve and watching the ball drop, as midnight strikes. Right at twelve, I looked out for the pumpkin carriage, which never came.

My brother Bill turned 71, which contributed to the party atmosphere. He is the only real Texan in our family, as he was born in Big Spring, Texas in 1949 on New Year's Eve.

But what is Texas? I was once on a small airplane going from Dallas to College Station, and a big, tall Texan got onto the airplane. His head nearly touched the ceiling. He sat down next to me, and I observed him order a whiskey. We sat and talked. He asked me where I was going, and I told him to a new position at Texas A&M University [TAMU]. He told me "I went there. You're going to the best university in the world. Where you're going is really the best public university in Texas, which happens to be in College Station." He was erudite. So, I said: "You're the perfect person to ask, where and what is Texas? Is it Southern?"

"No."

"Is it Midwestern?"

"No."

"I know it's not Northern or Eastern."

"You're correct."

"I know it's not Western."

"That's right."

"Well, we're going there, so where and what is it?"

He leaned back in his seat. Took a sip of his whiskey, and said slowly with a Texan drawl: "Texas is a state of mind." As we approached our destination. He said: "Look how beautiful it is, how developed. No where else will you find this kind of gothic military architecture." This description struck me as odd, but true.

However, it's no joke, I was at Texas A&M University for twenty-five years [1986–2011]. It sounds strange, that I would be at this flagship institution for higher learning for so long. However, it was the best job I ever had. It was the McMillan Professorship of Analytical Psychology, which was the first professorship of Jungian Psychology in the world. I also had an appointment in the medical school as Professor in the departments of Psychiatry and Humanities in Medicine.

I worked for 25 years as the McMillan Professor of Analytical Psychology at TAMU. One learns in academia that laughter in the classroom helps both professors and students. Surely this led to my being a standup comic later at the age of 70. If only Stephen Colbert had been in the audience! People can watch my performance on YouTube, titled "Dr. Nada Live at the Tiny Tavern."

It is serious business to write books. But, it is equally important to include humor, in whatever one does. So, I was thrilled to learn that Winston Churchill also utilized comedy. Once, a woman told Churchill "If you were my husband, I would give you poison," to which he replied, "If you were my wife, I'd take it."

I spent nearly a quarter of my life at Texas A&M University, where I was an Aggie. Of course, everyone knows what A&M stands for: "Analysis and Meditation," Right? Not really…the Aggies were based on tending the ground through agriculture as well as building things (as mechanics). Their rivals, the University of Texas, are called "Tea Sippers" insinuating that they were city folk. Truth be told, both universities embrace humor and academics. Examples of their rivalry: the Aggies would steal the Longhorn's mascot, a bull named Bevo, which was a difficult task. The Tea

Sippers would find and take Reveille, the dog mascot for the Aggies. It was surely easier to pull this one off.

Being an academic allowed me to research humor and wit. They are similar in that they both involve helping people to feel good, to laugh, giggle, or smile. On June 3, 2023, I gave a presentation in Eugene, Oregon to the Pacific Northwest Society of Jungian Analysts on the Healing Value of Humor in Analytic Treatment. Now, back to Texas…

In 1949, my father, also a physician, was working at the VA hospital in Big Spring, Texas. My dad moved us to Big Spring to work at this hospital. I recall watching TV (when I was four) with the babysitter who said, "Your brother was supposed to be the first baby of 1950 but ended up being the last baby of 1949!" You can see the connection between the baby and the babysitter. Possibly, she was considering or thinking about having a baby herself, since she was very excited about it. She was with me as we watched my younger brother come into this world – in a way, by giving me something to remember, she allowed me to glimpse his birth.

Chapter Four

Living in and with Nature

Two solitudes
end of the lane...
dream come true

Over the rise
Rattlesnake mountain...
Clarity

From my office window I can see Spencer Butte, or, as it was called originally by the Kalapuya Indians, Rattlesnake Mountain, a 2,100-acre ridgeline park system. This little poem was composed on the eve of 2021.

New Year's Day in 2021 was rainy. This rain meant that the drought was over, but it seemed too little too late. We expected that it would rain a lot in Oregon coming from Texas, but this new state, during such a hot summer and fall, did not live up to that.

The second day of 2021 produced another rain, heavier this time. Because of this the pond filled up with water. Often it rained, but I walked anyway and got wet. I did not let the rain keep me inside. It rained excessively and then got colder and began to snow in early January 2021.

On the sixth of January 2021, the US capitol was stormed. We're used to thinking of rain and storms, but this was a storm of people. Growing up, the idea of something like this was unthinkable, it was something that we figured would never happen. Yet, on January sixth, so many of us were shocked by the unthinkable becoming true. This upset me deeply. Later in the week, I had trouble believing that the riot at the Capitol had happened. I still do. Nothing like it, after all, had ever occurred before.

Moving away from that tragic event, and wanting to partake again in the things of everyday life, I took Alex, our sensitive caregiver, and his girlfriend Krissy to Ta Ra Rin for Thai cuisine on January 14th, and we had Tom Kha and Pad Thai. After dinner he and I went to Sundance Natural Foods for groceries and bought "Real Star Grapefruit" from Texas!

Alex has assisted me for nine years and originally, he wanted to do music therapy, most likely because he plays a mean guitar! However, he switched to counseling and now has his masters in it. Currently he works at a community-centered therapy clinic. Despite his busy schedule, he still maintains contact and helps me and Lanara on Fridays. Over the course of working together, we have become close friends – he's sort of like the son I never had. I say this because I never had an actual son. Imagine my happiness when Alex asked me to be the celebrant for his planned wedding with Krissy set for June 2024. Bringing together my love for nature and the beauty of Alex and Krissy's union, I have chosen to recite five traditional Native American prayers for the couple during their wedding.

Prayer #1

God in heaven above please protect the ones we love.
We honor all you created as we pledge our hearts and lives together.
We honor Mother Earth and ask for our marriage to be abundant and grow stronger through the seasons.
We honor fire and ask that our union be warm and glowing with love in our hearts.
We honor wind and ask that we sail through life safe and calm as we are in our father's arms.

We honor water to clean and soothe our marriage that it never thirsts for love.
We pray for harmony and true happiness as we forever grow young together.

Prayer #2

Powers of nature, we honor you. Protect these ones we love.
We honor mother earth and ask that their marriage be abundant and fruitful, growing stronger through the seasons.
We honor the wind and ask that they be lifted up to soar through life, safe and calm as in their fathers' arms.
We honor fire and ask that this union be warm and glowing with love in their hearts.
We honor water to cleanse and soothe this union that it may never thirst for love.
We honor all that is under the great sky as they pledge their hearts and lives.
Of all the powers of nature and the universe, we ask for harmony and happiness as they grow forever together.

Prayer #3

Now you feel no rain
for each of you will be shelter to the other.
Now you will feel no cold
for each of you will be warmth to the other.
There will be no loneliness for you.
Now you are two persons,
but there is only one life before you.
Go now to your dwelling place,
to enter into the days of your togetherness.
And may your days be good and long together.

Prayer #4

Beginnings, fresh and clean, part of the Sacred Wheel
Each morning is a new opportunity,
To share our love, our Souls, and Spirits,
With those who choose to Walk this Path along with us,
To learn the lessons of the Wheel, and grow closer,
To The One Who-Created-All.
Each day is fresh and unblemished, clean and pure.
Look around, Rejoice in the New Beginning,
The Sun rises again, our hearts beat within our bodies,
We draw fresh Breath, and re-enter the World.
Set aside the pain of past days, each day begins afresh,
Build upon the past, its lessons and joys,
Be strengthened by the love within,
Reach out in love to those around us.
For each day is a gift, given but once.

Prayer #5

Our Father, heaven dweller,
My loving will be (to) Thy name.
Your Lordship let it make its appearance.
Here upon earth let happen what you think,
The same as in heaven is done.
Daily our food give to us this day.
Forgive us our debts,
the same as we forgive our debtors,
And do not lead us into temptation but,
Deliver us from evil existing.
For thine your Lordship is,
And the power is,
And the glory is forever.
Amen

It's obvious why I picked these prayers because you can see how it applies to Krissy and Alex. These prayers allow us to realize that we are all the same, and that we want the same things. It makes me think of what Carl Jung said about Americans, that in every citizen is an American Indian. This is an example of the importance of ancestral heritage.

Here is a different and short Native American poem, this time by the Pawnee people (historically from Nebraska and Northern Kansas, but today in Oklahoma).

Earth our mother, breathe forth life
all night sleeping
now awaking
in the east
now see the dawn

Earth our mother, breathe and waken
leaves are stirring
all things moving
new day coming
life renewing

Eagle soaring, see the morning
see the new mysterious morning
something marvelous and sacred
though it happens every day
Dawn the child of God and Darkness

Lanara,queen of
organic gardens &
creative cooking

Little hope &
night light…
lots of love

As I often do over the New Year's holiday, I called my daughters. The first one I spoke with was Sarah [my oldest]. She was in

New Orleans with her sisters. I suggested to her that they enjoy jazz while there and go to Preservation Hall. Next, I talked with Laura and my youngest daughter Rachel and her partner Lia. As usual, all children are different. For instance, Sarah started the Phoenix Center outside of Austin, Texas for troubled children. Laura has worked for a pediatrician and helps young people save money. Rachel, on the other hand, is an educational consultant and teaches educators about the value of diversity.

As I've said, it rained quite a lot in January, which Lanara and I enjoyed. We love the sound on our tin roof and appreciate all the rainwater for our seasonal creek, and our trees and plants.

A former patient whom I talked with on the telephone in a distant state (Texas) told me that he had had Covid. He wasn't hospitalized, though, so that was good news. This prompted me to get my booster vaccine.

As we proceeded down the January trail, we ate at Royal India. Truth be told, Indian food is one of my favorites. I had an okra dish, Yum! When I got home, I walked the usual path through Lanara's garden and around the pond, something which I do nearly every day. At this time, I was working on my third memoir, "Finding Love and Life: Healing the Soul," which was released in 2023.

Lanara makes simple breakfasts of oatmeal, but for a treat, sometimes she adds scrambled eggs, toast and crisp bacon. As we all know, it's important to start each day with a good breakfast. If you are interested in more eatery tidbits, check out my cookbook: *The Alchemy of Cooking: Recipes with a Jungian Twist*. Speaking of breakfasts, and particularly those with a psychological bent, I have found it important to do without refined sugar. You might ask "why?", it's because this type of sugar leads to depression, which I learned from Larry Christensen, a researcher in nutritional psychology at Texas A&M University. In addition to no refined sugar, I do not consume dairy products, which was also recommended in a book called *The Wahls Protocol* written by a physician with MS.

Chapter Five

Every Day Is A Good Day

This chapter title was used as the title of a book that I published in 2020. So this is a concept that is dear to my heart, and I hope everybody's soul. This is a useful philosophy for one's life. If you think every day's a good day, you might live that way. And why not?

It can be rainy as is often the case, but it can also be dry. We live at the end of a lane that is paved at first, but quickly turns to gravel. When Lanara first told me about this place, there was a manufactured house on the site. She warned me that I wouldn't like the road or the place. She was right and wrong. She was right about the land and the area – I really did like it, and she does too. However, the manufactured house turned us off. It took us awhile to find Jack, who sold these things on a lot, to come and unscrew it, and take it on two semis out of here with his family and workers.

Lanara and I both love trees. In addition to the Red Bud that was here, she planted a Peach, Nectarine, Persimmon, Apricot, and two Apple trees. It feels like we now have a growing orchard of various fruit trees. It's comforting but strange to notice that all of the trees are naked in the winter, because the tall oaks and maples are so beautiful in their spring and summer growth.

In addition to these lovely fruit trees, I made sure there was a Gingko tree…why? Everywhere I've lived, I've made sure that there was a Gingko tree. This may not make sense to the reader, but it's important. How come? Because the Gingko tree is the oldest tree that exists. It's a little-known fact that the Gingko is over 200 million years old, the sole survivor of a genus of trees that existed before dinosaurs roamed the earth.

During this time my love of books was working overtime. I was writing *Opening Our Hearts* and *Waiting to Cross Over* -- which is what we're all doing. Both books of little poems were released in 2022. As collections of little poems, it was clear that poetry was on my mind, I was also working on memoir number three, "Finding Love and Life: Healing the Soul" which was published in 2023. Memoir number four, "Embracing the Sunset Years and Looking Ahead," which also was released in 2023.

On February 1st I walked around our place and Lanara made a sumptuous dinner of salmon cakes, broccoli, and sweet potatoes. I read "In the Shadows: Living and Coping with a Loved One's Chronic Illness" such as MS, It's sad …so sad.

On the night of February 11th, 2021, I had a strange dream: a demon was exorcized from my body. I woke up so shocked that I wrote it down immediately. A spiritual healer and others were gathered around me too, making this dream balanced. In sum, it was a spiritual experience. Dreams have been a way of understanding human life throughout history, they have been connected to religion for a long, long time. The veneration of nature has been something similar. Both nature and spirituality are intertwined, which may mean that nature and dreams have a particularly strong connection. The next day began the Year of the Ox following the Chinese calendar, symbolizing dependability, and hard work. It was also Abraham Lincoln's birthday. A quiet day and I bowed to him.

I dreamed of an Iranian girl soon after, whom I associated with my Goddaughter, Annahita Varahrami because she is of Iranian descent. This was a refreshing contrast to the demon dream. Annahita was one of my best students at Texas A&M in Psychology & Religious studies. When I needed an editorial assistant and secretary, I asked her if she would like to have such a job. She answered in the affirmative and became one of the best. I encouraged her to give her own presentation, which was accepted at a Religious Conference. She carried that out in an outstanding manner. She then went on to study Social Work as a graduate student at the University of Texas in Austin. Her first job was at IBM assisting staff with stress related issues. She is clearly an accomplished high achiever, as well as a gentle, supportive listener. It's noteworthy that after growing up with a Zoroastrian religion, Annahita then added Catholicism. Her father had passed away and when she asked me to be her Godfather, I was touched and thankful and so honored that I said "yes" immediately.

It was also during this time that I read the Gospel of Mary, a historical text brought back to life by Karen King from Harvard. She had to go find pieces of it in Egypt, Germany, all over the world, to put this gospel together. I cite the description of this book at length because of how important I feel the connection is between Mary Magdala and Jesus to be:

> Lost for more than fifteen hundred years, The Gospel of Mary is the only existing early Christian gospel written in the name of a woman. Karen L. King tells the story of the recovery of this remarkable gospel and offers a new translation. This brief narrative rejects Jesus' suffering and death as a path to eternal life and exposes the view that Mary Magdalene was a prostitute for what it is--a piece of theological fiction. "The Gospel of Mary of Magdala" offers a fascinating glimpse into the conflicts and controversies that shaped earliest Christianity.

At one point in the book, Mary has a confrontation with Peter, in which she says (to Peter's interpretation of Jesus' philosophy) "That's not right, I knew Him, what He said, and what He stood for." I believe that most Christians would just throw this book away, because of how shocking some of its points might be. However, as an academic, I highly recommend this scholarly text.

Cool wind
pushes away the storm…
light breeze

This little poem underscores the title of this chapter because who would have thought that a mild breeze could push away a storm. This is important information to keep in mind when something bad happens. Take the time to see the good in it.

Valentine's day 2021 is ushered in, which I have always liked, and still do, thanks to my dear wife. I got Lanara a beautiful card. She also got me a lovely card. However, the best thing was that Lanara agreed to be my Valentine forever. As I neared my 76th birthday, I thought of others who were approaching a similar age, like Steve Martin. I will never forget his Little Shop of Horrors movie, which is about having a reluctance to go to the dentist (something which we all must deal with). But his little shop of horrors was a floral shop with carnivorous plants.

We had regular visits to King Estate during this time-period (winery and restaurant, where you can sit on the patio, have an excellent meal, seeing all the grapes you can drink later – great food). Their wine is shipped all over the country and the world.

When Rachel visited, she was pregnant. That made her, Lia and her future grandparents proud. When Ember was born a few months later it made all of us happy, and we thanked the Supreme Being for sending her to us. Rachel visited on her own and we had an early dinner at the Excelsior restaurant. Rachel gave me a "Papa Bear" mug and a keychain for my birthday. It was very nice. I use my mug every day with my coffee and tea. And my keychain goes with me on a daily basis. Rachel gave Lanara a break for a retreat, which she enjoyed. Lanara returned home safely, thank Yahweh and Sofia! Then Rachel returned to Texas after keeping me company during Lanara's vital time away.

Rebekah Sinclair began assisting with my 3rd memoir, "Finding Love and Life: Healing the Soul," which wasn't published until 2023. During this time Alex was also coming 4 times a week, as my Caregiver. I had nearly fallen in the bathroom, I didn't, but it scared me. I was able to grab the handrail bar to catch myself.

Chapter Six

Meeting a Goddess
in a Far-Off Land

It was 2005, when I met Lanara in New Zealand on a bench overlooking Governors Bay at the Allendale Reserve, which is what we call a Park. I was 60 and she was 49. It was love at first sight. When one grows in love, it is natural for marriage to follow. In 2009 when I was 64 and Lanara was 53 our wedding took place in Springfield, Oregon. Why the city across the Willamette River from Eugene, Oregon? Lane County, which is our home, at that time had stopped doing civil ceremonies.

Ironically, I had just been diagnosed with MS by a neurologist, Dr. Joan Jensen, on the day of my wedding to Lanara in 2009. During the diagnosis Dr. Jensen said, looking at my startled reaction: "Don't worry, there are treatments." Those early treatments involved injections of glatiramer acetate (known by its brand-name as Copaxone), which modifies certain immune processes responsible for MS. The person who developed this treatment, the first certified for use in MS patients, was Ruth Arnon – an Israeli immunologist, biologist, and chemist. It's time to thank her, and it's probably the reason why I am surviving so long, although the recommended additional treatments of regular massage and acupuncture were also helpful. But, to be honest and clear, it is love.

After seeing Joan, I went home to tell Lanara the news: I said, "You don't have to marry me, if you don't want to." She said, "It makes no difference." I was deeply touched and moved, I realized how much I wanted to marry her. And, we have remained true to our vows, in particular: to loving each other in sickness and in health.

My lovely wife is skilled at designing and picking artwork that works in specific places. In our new home in the country, it's meaningful that we chose part of a framed wedding dress given to me by Naoko Nakamura, which I have included below.

When I was going to Japan during one of my three visits there, I supervised a woman psychologist. This woman was Naoko Nakamura. My heart feels good because she eventually became a Jungian psychoanalyst. My last time with her was in the Kyoto train station when she brought me a gift. I said that I could not take it onto the airplane because of the glass. She said: "No worries, I'll send it to you." This framed part of a wedding gown was found in a dresser of a bombed-out home in Tokyo during World War II. It belonged to the grandmother of Naoko Nakamura. In case one doesn't know, that fire-bombing of Tokyo was as destructive as the atomic bombing of Hiroshima, resulting in just as many deaths. Naoko told me, "Put it up in your home, because I know you'll tell people the whole story." Honoring Naoko and her grandmother, I did what she wanted me to do.

Burning candles/hope in the/badlands

Autumn…
catch a leaf
by its stem

Under a peach tree…
glimpse of
heaven

Chapter Seven

Blueberries and Poetry

Blueberries encompass our feelings and our love of berries (whether they're strawberries or blueberries). I even feel the same way about gooseberries if they are ripe. Blueberries have the blues. Unlike strawberries which are red like Mars, a person who is a bit melancholic, like me, prefers blueberries. But as I mentioned above, there are always gooseberries to liven the day, particularly if they are ready to eat. They even grow in Oregon, as "yellowish-green" Champion Berries – these will soon be added to our garden. Blueberries are close to the heart of a melancholic soul; however, the Champion ones look promising. In any case, one might find the mood of a blueberry in the following poem.

> Imagine if all people said like Natsume Soseki:[1] "Every day's a good day"?
> We don't usually think this way—
> but why not?
>
> Is it because of Putin, and the war in Ukraine?
> Or can we go beyond that,
> to Poetry, and the imagined.
>
> Or is it just pain in general?

1. Soseki (1867–1916) was a Japanese novelist who also became a Buddhist monk.

Or specifically, like I have, MS?

When I wrote this I was 75, happily married –
but falling apart…not yet. I'm 78 and despite being ill, it's a
lovefest with Lanara.
Why do I say happily married and that it's a lovefest?
Because if you were married to Lanara you'd probably say the
same thing.
She's a great cook, as well as a nature goddess. She is smart
about many things, such as
gardening and mythology. She is also beautiful, kind, giving
and loving. When I met her in New
Zealand, she was cooking for orphans. Since our parents are
deceased, she continues to cook
for orphans. And, she loves herself and me with my condition.
Lanara clearly is a lovely human
being. She honors our wedding vows that we made fourteen
years ago and on our meeting
eighteen years ago in New Zealand on its South Island.

Thank the Lord and Sophia for Lanara.
Okay, she has more than a beauty spot…
She is, giving, sensitive, curious, and bright.
Lanara is my dear wife, but more importantly, my best friend.
It's August in Oregon and Lanara's garden is lovely.
There are some blueberries, which the birds have not eaten.
And there are also strawberries that are delicious and thrive
here.
Plus, we have two apple trees, a plum tree as well as a persim-
mon tree, that all do well.

I wanted to use some words in this poem, so here they are:
Talent, creativity, risk, curiosity, love, and passion.

We don't usually think this—
but why not?

Okay, I'll share one of Lanara's recent little poems. Yes, she is
also a poet:

Embracing the Sunset Years and Looking Ahead

Big ocean
hushes and sand…
restless mind

As we know, the ocean calms a busy mind.

Both Lanara and Alex have helped me to live a full life. Alex helped me with typing memoir three, as Nick is doing with memoir four. James Miller Jr. has also helped me by assisting with typing and editing. And James wrote an outstanding Foreword to my 3rd memoir, "Finding Love and Life: Healing the Soul," which was released in 2023. He also stays with me at night, as do other altruistic caregivers, specifically Rene Good and Tina Smith

On February 25th 2021, I turned 76. The next day it rained, and I loved walking in the rain. A dinner of Texas Bar B Que sent to us by my daughters. Then I had a tearful talk with Lanara about how hard it is for her to care for me. I said that I was sorry that I was ill…so sorry. It hurts me to know that I am a burden on her. It then gently rained. The slow rain is like God crying.

Settling into
darkness…
moonlight appears.

On March 10,2021 I dreamt of wealthy relatives in New York City. I didn't understand what this meant at first, but it helped me to later realize that wealth means more than money. The life these relatives were living was and is totally foreign to me, as is N.Y.C.

It could be meaningful and represent that Lanara and I would actualize a dream that we had when we first met in 2005. At that time, eighteen years ago in New Zealand, we had a mutual goal of living together in the country at the end of a gravel road in our own unique house. This dream has, amazingly, came true.

When thinking back on how far I've come, sitting at our oval, Amish table, I reflect on my work to understand myself through seeing Freudian, Kleinian, and Jungian psychoanalysts. Freud, everybody knows, and it's critical to resolve the issue of wanting to consummate with your mother and kill your father. In part, this might be true, but you don't actually want to do that. So, I moved on to Klein, who underscored play, which we all like and don't do enough of as adults. It's noteworthy that Melanie Klein established her own psychology, but originally wanted to be a medical doctor. However, her healing ways are like the ideals of Hippocrates. She believed that play was central to mental health and revealed unconscious material similarly to free association and dreams. This was her link to Sigmund and Anna Freud. So, the inner child in all adults needs to be reached and joined with, which was a focus of Melanie Klein, as well as Carl Jung and Donald Winnicott. Jung's concept of active imagination results in artistic products, things like play, or writing a play or memoir. There are many activities that could become realized through active imagination: some patients write, draw or paint, while others use ceramics or even dance.

In early March, Rebekkah was not coming to assist me with typing, so I went to see Deborah Vukson for a Feldenkrais treatment. This kind of treatment integrates neural and-muscular interactions and is extremely helpful for people like me. After arriving home, I walked with Alex around the garden paths, observing Lanara's vegetable and floral plantings. I talked with Rachael & Lia by phone to apologize that we were unable to attend their wedding. We then called my Grandson, Aidan to wish him a Happy 18th Birthday! His life's goal is to become a filmmaker. If he is committed and persistent, he will manifest his dream.

Happy Easter! I again called my daughters, which I always do around this special holiday. At this time Lanara went for her Spring break holiday at a cabin in the woods, something which is essential for her to do periodically. While she was gone Alex and I went to Sushi Domo, which we really like to go to for Japanese food. I had my usual California roll, miso soup, and salad. Alex got a special combination plate, with several rolls.

On April 8th I met with Jimmy and Jim at a Thai restaurant. Jimmy, or James Stock, founded Wipf and Stock Publishers and Jim Tedrick oversees all the books as an editor in chief. This relationship with a small press is unusual. Looking back to my career as a writer, in New York City I recall being given coffee at a major press like Penguin, and I didn't know anything about the people who ran the business. So, the feeling of having a personal connection with Wipf and Stock is very different.

I like to read poetry. I found and reread William Carlos Williams poem "The Red Wheelbarrow": So much depends/upon/a red wheelbarrow/glazed with rainwater/beside the white/chickens. Inspired by his poem, I wrote a "Blue Walker" one. My life depends/on a blue walker/moving slowly/through the gate/around the pond/a cougar watches. For any reader who does not know about William Carlos Williams, he was a pediatrician who wrote plays, essays, and poetry. He considered himself a common person, and wanted to write something that those unfamiliar to poetry could connect with. Coming from his work as a physician to children – having to be able to reach them, as well as their parents – he seemed to have a skill for speaking and writing in approachable language. Most likely his work helped him to develop his inner child and allowed it to grow up and extend out in the world.

George Gershwin, another talented and creative individual who tapped into his inner child, unfortunately died from a brain-tumor. Gershwin was able, like Williams, to reach many kinds of people with his art, introducing jazz through symphonic music to those unfamiliar, and especially to children (who loved Gershwin). Of course, this would have reached not only children, but all individuals, showing how the inner child plays a crucial part in the making of music and poetry. As American modernists, both William Carlos Williams and George Gershwin felt themselves to be men "without traditions," which allowed them to express their essential being through creative works.[2]

Wind spirits…
birds flying
in holy circles

2. Oja, Carol J. "Gershwin and American Modernists of the 1920s." *The Musical Quarterly,* vol. 78, 1994.

Chapter Eight

Personal History, Spirituality and Analysis

A favorite grandfather was my mother's dad, Karl Middendorf, who was a civil engineer, and a damn good writer. He wrote a private memoir about his family that I was always impressed with. This may be where the memoir seed came from. Karl's family had Germanic roots. Maybe this is why I took three years of German and German literature at the University of California, Berkeley.

On May 6th I dreamt of an old family home in Berlin that was taken over by Nazis. Some were helpful. My associations were: how my visits to Berlin were overall positive, even when the city was split between West and East. However, as part Jewish, I was hurt by the discrimination against Jews in World War II. When I entered East Germany, I was 18 years old and a student at the University of Copenhagen. I wanted to see for myself what it was like behind the Iron Curtain in East Germany. At the Checkpoint Charlie they asked me what I was going to do, and I told them that I would be walking around – they told me to be careful. Not long after that I saw a woman walking down the street. I asked her if she could tell me more about what it was like to live in East Germany, because I suspected that some of its US characterization was propaganda. We introduced ourselves, her name was Ruth. She told me sure, and led me to her apartment, which was half of a floor in an apartment building. I was shocked to see that it was quite nice – though we had to walk up because there was no elevator. When we entered, she made a hushing sign, whispering to me that her kids were sleeping. First she opened the door to the room where her two pre-teen children, a boy and a girl, were laying on a mattress on the floor. I met her husband Siegfried in their living room, who, after serving me coffee, asked me what I was doing in East Germany. I told him that I wanted to see what the Communist countries were really like, because we had such propaganda that citizens there were suffering and living in terrible places. Siegfried said: "Well now you can see that's not true." He added, "Hopefully, in the future, we will all be able to accept each other and relate peacefully." Parenthetically, Siegfried was a high official in the East German government. Leaving those memories behind, I return to the present time in Oregon.

We have a mock orange, a healthy, vibrant shrub, which in the Spring pairs well with our Oregon sunshine flowers.[1]

1. I credit both of these pictures to the Portland Nursery in Oregon.

Mock orange blossoms &
Oregon sunshine
like the sun

I love *Growing Up*, a book by Russell Baker, but quickly realized that I'm growing down. However, the key word is "growing." This process of growth and development even led me to re-enter Jungian analysis at a late age. I decided to see Jim Soliday, a Jungian analyst that I liked a lot, and interestingly (because we had dinner along with our annual Jungian meetings) Lanara got the chance to meet him, and liked him. He was a former minister who had this unique background in religion, which is not uncommon for Jungian analysts. I began to see him on July 27th, 2021. My initial question was "Why me, O Lord?" Was it fate, or destiny? Fate is not what happens to us, but how we handle it. Destiny is when we wake up, and have to deal with it. Fate is something we are dealt, but destiny we have some control over. In other words, we all have crosses to bear, and we have limitations to our freedom, but perhaps our agency lies between the two. It's like Jung's theory of the Self, which represents totality and wholeness, and the ego is secondary to it, which allows the person (with the Lord and Sophia helping) to figure out their own personal myth.

What is one's personal myth? It's when the individual glimpses and figures out that they are here for a special reason. It's not to work for some big company or university, but to be his or her unique self. This is surely helpful when approaching the afterlife. In Buddhism, there is a 'Sagga' (Heaven), which, interestingly, has two levels of higher existence through which one can become reborn. This sounds a lot like the highest level of consciousness which Jung called the Self. To get to this place one must recognize the secondary position of the ego.

I was trying to figure out why I developed MS at the age of 64, which is why I contacted Jim Soliday in the first place. At this point, I realized that this was the cross I had to bear, and it's noteworthy that where we live in the country there are bears all around. Bears are vegetarian, usually. They like to pick berries and eat them. However, if there's a drought (like the current situation) they will eat almost anything. This makes me think of a time when I went on a retreat at a monastery, when one day, a bear opened the door to the kitchen and took a big plastic jar of the monks' peanut butter. Nobody had any peanut butter and jelly sandwiches that week – this was one way of getting close to the Lord.

This monastery was called Our Lady of Guadalupe, in Pecos, New Mexico, and it was just contiguous to a nunnery (and a large ranch owned by Jane Fonda). Every Wednesday night the monastery opened their doors for a public prayer night. One evening I remember this couple coming in: a monk and a nun who had married from that very location. I was astounded, but happy for them. The appearance of this former nun, and her confidence to do precisely what she wanted, reminded me how excited I was, and pleased that Jane Fonda went to North Vietnam, and had a hand in ending the war. Fonda actually had a practical relationship with this monastery, she would ask the monks for certain kinds of labor to be done on her ranch.

I was also introduced to life at a monastery when I was at the University of Rochester. While speaking with a chaplain at the university medical center, who was part of the consultation team that I headed (psychiatric, medical, nursing, psychological, social-work, and religious / spiritual) I mentioned that I had always wanted to visit a monastery. To this he told me that I could go to "Our Lady of the Genesee" in Piffard, New York. I went there alone over the Christmas and New Year holidays, which meant nobody else was around. Alone is important, as it derives from "All One." It was there that I developed my theory of "Egocide and Transformation," because I was undergoing that process for myself through a stay at the monastery. When I got there, I met the Abbot John Eudes Bamberger. Since we were both psychiatrists, he met me when I began my visit. After we walked to a small room together, he told me that his duty involved traveling to different monasteries and checking whether the monks joining their Trappist institutions were psychologically healthy. He later mentioned that they made bread on site, and offered me a loaf of Monk's Bread, either white, whole wheat, or raisin. I went with the raisin. It was interesting and meaningful that I had chosen a place that had an abbot who had been educated by Thomas Merton at the Abbey of Our Lady Gethsemani Monastery. Merton's popular autobiography *The Seven Storey Mountain* had deeply impacted me and many others.

"Love the life you live &
live the life you love."
[Thanks Bob Marley]

Thinking about how these interests of mine are linked together, I have viewed Jung's psychology as spiritual, philosophical, and related to my personal journey. Let me take you into the first session with my late Jungian analyst, Jim Soliday. I say this because he passed away shortly after I stopped seeing him. I was impressed that Jim had read many of my books, so he knew me in that way, which is probably why I wanted to see him (without knowing it). He listened very well, and told me that the dark material I spoke of was important, that I should hold onto it and let it evolve. I liked this idea, and believed that I should write partly from that place of darkness. We spoke about the importance of nature, and its connection to my last name, which means roses. I recall that important analytic session where I said to him "Illness brought me into wholeness." We discussed Jung's work on the creative illness. This visit planted a seed for me to begin to accept MS as a part of my life. Of course, I was upset by being ill, however, it led me to reflect on its value. Even in some books I've written about what MS means to me, as follows: my star, my shrink, my survivor, my sanity, my silence, my setback, my sanctuary, my suffering.

One thing that linked Jim and me was our mutual experience in teaching and mentoring. Both of our understandings of Jung were impacted by music. When I had written the *Tao of Elvis*, he wasn't surprised, like some were, but was curious about it, probably because of his experience teaching (with Bob Stuckey) the history of rock and roll. Jim was a kind soul.

Recently I saw a physical therapist who I had seen before to help me with a range of motion therapies. I sensed that she was different, more empathic, and authentic. She had survived brain cancer since I had last seen her, and Lanara and I believed that, like me, illness had brought her into wholeness. It impressed us that even while suffering, she continued helping others. This, too, reminds me of Jung's "Creative illness."

Horace Walpole once said that "the world is a tragedy to those who feel, but a comedy to those who think." I am both a feeling and thinking type, so it makes sense to me that I eventually felt comfortable doing comedy, which I performed on July 31st 2014. This reminds of my previous disclosure, that I have done my own comedic performances in Eugene, Oregon: "Dr. Nada Live at the Tiny Tavern." However, Lanara said that I've been doing comedy ever since she met me, and probably all my life. I thought, wow! -- that's true, people have been laughing at things I've said since I was a boy. She said that happened to her too, as a girl, but she never wanted to perform.

In my elderly analysis Jim helped me realize that it took courage to ask for help. Hence, I was no longer stuck, which is how Jung viewed depression. I was rediscovering the beauty of roses. This all leads me to suspect, following Goethe's book *The Sorrows of Young*

Werther (1787), that my breakout novel would be *The Sorrows and Joys of Old Rosen*. That book relates to my concept of egocide and transformation. Werther liked a woman who rebuffed him, and so grappled with what it meant to be rejected by a lover. Werther's eventual death (by his own hand) allowed Goethe to work through what I imagine was his own suicidal complex in a creative way. Another example of autobiographical self-reflection and healing is the work by Donald Murray. I agree with Murray, who was himself a prolific writer, that all writing is autobiographical.[2]

I also thought about what Goethe said when he was dying: "More light." Having MS has brought me dark days, but I agree with Goethe's philosophy that it's also brought me much light. I've sorted out important life issues. It's like Jung's concept of "Death and Rebirth." For many individuals, having MS would have led to serious chronic illness and impending death. However, with me, it's brought me more creativity than I ever could have imagined. It's also caused me to ask for help from doctors, nurses, physical therapists, and caretakers. I've shared and associated to my dreams and sought the meaning of them. I dreamt of Great Britain and my studies, profession and travel. My associations were that I spent time as a medical student and psychiatric resident in Edinburgh, Scotland and later as a faculty member in Edinburgh and London, as well as Zurich, Switzerland. Then I carried out a research project with Deborah Voorhees in the Shetland Islands. It involved studying the impact of North Sea Oil discoveries and developments on the health and mental health of Shetlanders. For example, the largest oil port In Europe was built in the Shetland Islands to accommodate big ships to transport the oil to refineries and storage facilities away from the Shetland Islands. At that time, bringing the oil ashore, if they were a country, the Shetland Islands would have been the 5th largest oil producing nation in the world. The Shetland County government worked out an agreement with the oil companies, like Shell and BP for disturbance monies of 50 million pounds. This ended up being a godsend for this remote

2. Murray, Donald. "All Writing is Autobiography." *College, Composition, and Communication*, vol. 42, no. 1, 1991.

group of islands. For example, on the main island, they were able to construct an indoor covered football field, basketball court and an Olympic sized heated swimming pool. They also used some of these funds to enhance their own language and culture. In addition, these funds supported community centers and local activities such as sports, plays and other after school activities. In other words, they used the disturbance monies wisely.

Many ideas came to fruition, for example, I was involved in helping my soul and soulful activities. For instance, our first daughter, Sarah, was born in the Shetland Islands in 1976. Going to New Zealand reminded me of the Shetland. They both are agriculturally based, but close to the sea. These islands included timber and lovely beaches, as well. Another parallel was their reliance on fishing. I hope oil isn't discovered of the coast of New Zealand, but it could happen. If oil is discovered, New Zealand would parallel the Shetland Islands in the control of it. They are very independent regions, which is to their credit. New Zealand has developed wind power which already generates 6% of their electricity. This would also work in windy Shetland.

Both Shetland and New Zealand have rolling hills in common, as well as the sea, with waves always rolling in and rolling out. Riding a rollercoaster provides some of the same enlightenment. We all know how fun it is to ride, as the rollercoaster goes slowly up this huge hill, and then *down, fast!* (thank God we're locked in). And we enjoy the ride, and scream. It sounds like life. What do I mean by this? When I was young, I would have never thought that I'd write a book. But having attended the Antioch Writer's Conference in 1990, I came out of that educational gathering as a writer, despite not knowing that it was my destiny. However, the seeds were there, as all academics must write. When you have papers accepted, you get the sense that maybe your writing is good. Then come books. The other practical aspect that helped me was advice from Clarissa Pinkola Estés who was a fellow colleague trained to be a Jungian analyst. She wrote "Women Who Run with the Wolves." We both loved writing, so I asked her "How do I get a book published?" She told me that all I needed was a good agent.

She recommended Ned Levitt, someone who was her agent. So, I contacted him, and it worked. Ned became my agent for two of my books "Egocide and Transcendence" which became "Transforming Depression: Healing the Soul through Creativity" and "The Tao of Jung: Integrity in Depth." He told me how it works with agents: they go to a meeting where editors and agents are together. Then they share proposals that they have gotten for books. Several people told him he should publish "this one," which was my manuscript for *Transforming Depression: Healing the Soul Through Creativity*. Later on at the Antioch Writer's Conference, a different agent asked what I was currently working on, and I told him it was *The Tao of Jung: The Way of Integrity*. He said that book would be purchased just for the title! And that was true.

Chapter Nine

Reflecting On How Fortunate
I Am

Beads of
charming friendship,
around my neck

Ever since I met Lanara in 2005 on a bench in New Zealand, she
has been a unique and special person in my life. When I saw her on
the bench, I asked if she would scoot over, because I had brought
my lunch to eat by Governors Bay. It took her awhile to respond.
Later I learned that she was looking at my fingernails. So, I passed
the test. Many of my poems to this day are related to her and our
special union. We got married in 2009 in Oregon, where we had
moved from Texas. After I formally retired from TAMU in 2011, I
became an Affiliate Professor in Psychiatry at OHSU.

The following little poems are about Lanara and in her honor:

Deep
and lasting love . . . Marriage is a garden of love
New Zealand

What you
give me
beyond words

I love you…
always have
always will

Eyes closed,
heart open…
multitude of stars

I bow to the
tall fir trees,
reaching skyward

Misty, golden path…
eternity

In early August of 2021 Lanara left for one of her regular re-treats, which she deserves for taking care of me. I cried, as I love her so much. Before she left for Yachats, a rugged and charming town on Oregon's beautiful coast, she made oatmeal, which I like as much as I liked Cream of Wheat as a boy. She called as soon as she got there, which is one of our agreements. The cabin had an outside redwood container in which warm spring water flowed. Her description reminded me of the natural Onsen pools in Japan which are hot water springs. I used to immerse myself in them in that country.

Eating out, especially with foreign foods, is a joy. For example, on August 4th, Alex and I went to Royal India, as it is a real treat. The next day was quiet, warm, but not hot. I walked as usual. Our grapes were growing and thriving and well on their way to being picked.

In my journal, I noted my dreams as well as my active imagi-nation. I dreamt that I was with a woman, I said "I love you" to her, and she reciprocated. She had a dark complexion and I realized that she represented my anima. She was strong and dark like I am. There was a loving relationship between us. The anima is necessary for all creative work, so this dream made me happy. On August 9th, I drew a group of circles, with a snake-serpent approaching. What this meant to me, with the four concentric circles, was that I was in contact with the feminine, or the anima, especially as the number of circles (an even four) was feminine too. Men, on the other hand, are represented by squares.[1] Jung, in his brilliance, saw the feminine part of a man as circular, and critical for creativity. The healing nature is to actualize both. One example of integrating both could be a medical doctor who practices the art and science of medicine, which is something I describe in *Soul to Soul: Aphorisms for Life*. A successful writer must integrate both as well. And being a doctor and writer, I am doubly blessed! The snake is a symbol of healing, which is utilized in the famous rod of Asclepius (a rod with a serpent intertwined around it), the Greco-Roman god of medicine, nursing, and all healing.

A cloud still

then it moves…

so slowly

I dreamt of a woman who was fond of a baby sloth. This was the mascot for some institution, perhaps a graduate institute like Pacifica, a place where Jungian psychology is routinely taught. Historically, Clarissa Pinkola Estés and I applied to be co-directors at Pacifica, but the owner refused us both, and selected Joe Cambray as the head. Steven Eisenstat, the owner, wanted Pacifica to be represented by one person. This was a good choice, in a way, because Joe encompasses both. At this interview between myself and Eisenstat, I accidentally dribbled soup on my tie, which may have cost me the job. He said, "That was sloth-like." This was a strange comment and cemented in my mind that I really did not want to work there. In another dream, I learned of a mascot at Pacifica which was a new baby. This probably is why I referred people to Pacifica, because a baby, often in a dream, represents hope and new life. I had also been a Visiting Professor there in the past when I was the McMillan Professor of Analytical Psychology at TAMU.

---

1. Schott, G. D. *National Library of Medicine: National Center for Biotechnology Information*. "Sex Symbols Ancient and Modern: Their Origins and Iconography on the Pedigree." December 2005. https://www.ncbi.nlm.nih.gov/pmc/articles/PMC1322246/

On September 22nd, 2021 I was on a podcast called *Speaking of Jung*, developed by Laura London, who was a wonderful interviewer. *Speaking of Jung* is a brilliant series which broadcasts interviews of Jungian analysts. She interviewed Frank McMillan III who recommended that she interview me, because I had held the McMillan Professorship of Analytical Psychology at TAMU. London had read my books and I felt she knew just what to ask me. "Transforming Depression : Healing the Soul through Creativity," which I show below was first published by Putnam, but was eventually picked up by Penguin. This book is still in print with a small publishing company called Nicolas-Hays. This book was translated into Chinese. I was once interviewed by a group of readers of this book from China through the computer. It was a heartwarming and intelligent conversation, and I was pleased that this book and my concepts would help the people in China.

Embracing the Sunset Years and Looking Ahead

On October 14th, 2021, I had a dream that seemed to pass by in a flash. It's unusual for me to wake up remembering only an image, but that was what happened. It was so strange to see an old man with a beard, something associated with both depression and knowledge. In the dream the man was called Dr. Sage. I looked up sage, because I had written about him and I was struck by its strangeness. And I discovered that it was associated with wisdom and age. It's also used for cleansing negative energy. So, I am left with this quandary of whether I could really be wise. Sages are also related to myth and legend, which recalls Jung's collective unconscious. It was striking, too, that I chose to go back into analysis as an old man with an older man. Jim Soliday was 80 and I was 76 when we began meeting. Because of our shared old age and his kindness, he was able to help me with the acceptance of my illness and becoming older.

The shadow is the negative part of the ego, which my interest in suicide has attracted me towards. I once asked James Hillman if he wanted to do a panel with me on suicide, the reason being because he had written a book called *Suicide and the Soul*. He told me that he had already dealt with that – shocked, I wondered whether something like suicide could ever be fully dealt with. Hillman had confronted his own shadow, so that he could say *no* to suicide. We were doing similar kinds of work. Hillman was a very controversial figure in Jungian psychology. He used to be the Director of Education at the Jung Institute in Zurich. Later he set up his own training program. However, it seemed that he was fixated on his image and archetypal imagination. He once delivered a lecture called "On Betrayal," a very good speech, which was published, in which he seems to confront his shadow. In his case of a negative father complex, which is illustrated by this passage from that lecture:

> "There is a Jewish story, an ordinary Jewish Joke. It runs like this: A father was teaching his little son to be less afraid, to have more courage, by having him jump down the stairs. He placed his boy on the second stair and said, "Jump, and I'll catch you." and the boy jumped. Then the

father placed him on the third stair, saying "Jump, and I'll catch you." Though the boy was afraid, he trusted his father, did what he was told, and jumped into his father's arms. Then the father put him on the next step, and the next step, each time telling him, Jump, and I'll catch you, and each time the boy jumped and was caught by his father. And so this went on. Then the boy jumped from a very high step, just as before; but this time the father stepped back, and the boy fell flat on his face. As he picked himself up, bleeding and crying, the father said, "That will teach you: never trust a Jew, even if it's your own father."[2]

I respected James Hillman's intellect but was wary of this side of his personality. Nor was I alone. Criticisms of his behavior have leaked out in conversations around me. Despite this, he was a key figure in the Inter-Regional Society of Jungian Analysts. I was told by the search committee for the McMillan Professorship at Texas A&M University, that they had received his resume, but ultimately found it unsatisfactory. Hillman was, in a way, larger than life, and sought control over his life by attaching his name to an Institute he himself had founded.

On November 4th, 2021, I spoke again with Jim Soliday. He understood what I was saying about Lanara needing a break from caring for me – so Jim clearly had empathy. It's hard for me with increased weakness, but I still walk every day, though it's difficult.

On December 2nd I dreamt that I was in China at a conference, and that I went to see a movie. There was a long line. When I got to the ticket window, I bought seven tickets. Why seven? It's a number of completion and it also means holy. What did I do? I gave the rest of the tickets to the next six people in line. This made me curious about what seven meant. Jacob once spoke about seven tribes of Israel, but today there are 12 recognized historical tribes. However, this led me to want to write a new book on synchronicity and wisdom. However, this changed to synchronicity and individuation when I decided to write about CG Jung and his

2. Hillman, James. "On Betrayal." *Guild of Pastoral Psychology*, lecture delivered on October 2nd, 1964.

analytical psychology. *Synchronicity and Individuation* was similar to my book *Soul to Soul* in size and style. Both books are about heart and soul. I was also working on my third memoir *Finding Love and Life: Healing the Soul*, which was published in 2023.

Reflecting on China, I went to a conference there in 1998. It was actually true, what I had seen and read about China: the hills looks like they do in many Chinese paintings. At a lunch meeting at this conference, an American student sat next to me. I said: "what are you doing here?" He said: "I emigrated here." I said: "Really?" He said: "Yeah, I discovered that being here, I get housing, healthcare, and education for free. All they require of me is that I fulfill my dream of *being* educated here."

January of 2022 began with freezing weather and snow, though it melted quickly. On January 6th, I had an upsetting dream about killing old people. This represents a part of myself that attacks me – the part of me which does not like to be elderly. I'm 76 and Jim is 80, and he is like a brother. Dealing with ageism is difficult, especially with this interior self which wants to kill them. But Jim said: "Dave, wake up! You are old. The collective is hateful, but helpful. The culture is anti-ageing, just deal with it."

On January 8th Lanara left on one of her trips to Yachats, Oregon. Sarah visited then, but I had trouble sleeping. I needed to sleep! Despite knowing the obvious, I had difficulty. It's always been a comfort to observe my daughter Sarah's painting. She is a fine artist, who went to University of Texas in Austin to study art, and you can see what resulted in this painting:

My youngest daughter, Rachel, also paints. Art is a big part of all of our lives. January 27th 2022 my daughter Rachel had her first baby, my dear granddaughter, Ember Jean Rosen. She was and is cute ,smart, creative and healthy. I have learned recently that my first granddaughter also likes art, although she's only nearly two.

As I began February, I also began writing my third memoir, *Finding Love and Life: Healing the Soul.* This was eventually published in 2023.

Alone
allows one to be
all one

Reflecting on these words helped me to realize that "alone" is such an American, individualistic philosophy, but really, it's about being One with the Supreme Being. Spinoza is a favorite philosopher of mine because he would have understood this little poem. Spinoza's interpretation of *all* things enveloped by *one* substance shows how interrelated being alone can be. Flash back. In 1963, when I was 19, I studied at the University of Copenhagen. It was an enlightening experience because I learned how valuable socialistic ideas can be. For example, I asked the family I was staying with where the slums were in that city. They told me: "We don't have those here." I told them I had never been to city that didn't have slums. "Well that's America," they said, "Here we make sure that everybody has a good place to live, a job, and great education." This is all guaranteed by their constitution. Homes are given to the homeless. I was heartened to find out from my Danish family that everybody could have a good home, a job, and an education. For example, when I would get onto the bus, or the tram, in Copenhagen, the driver would always address me in perfect English – this was how successful their educational system was. Whereas here, if there were a Chinese visitor on our bus system, most bus drivers would not be able to speak their language.

February 25th, my 77th birthday and a realization: I've seen and done a lot. When my kids were little, they used to ask me "What does MD mean?" I would say "My Daddy," only later did they learn that it stood for Medical Doctor.

However, most artists and philosophers have done a lot too: Just consider Marilyn Monroe, Elvis Presley, Wolfgang Goethe and Seren Kierkegaard.

March 3rd 2022 was my 9th and final session with Jim Soliday, so I reflected on all the therapy that I've had: Freudian, Kleinian, and Jungian. At this point, I realized that I don't really need, or want any more therapy. Saying that caused me to pinch myself, because any of us can always use therapy. So upon reflection, it's something I should remain open to just in case.

It was on a Wednesday, March 22nd 2022, that I found out Jim Soliday had died, because that was the day we normally spoke. I was told that he had died 7 days earlier, on March 19th. I was sad from this news, because I thought that our analytic process was going well, and because of our close relationship. Lanara and I sent his dear wife Kay a card of condolences. Jim will be missed by myself, my wife, and truly all the people who knew him.

On March 23rd, my doorbell was rung, but no one was there. From a purely logical perspective, it's almost unbelievable. However, this was the day that Jim and I were supposed to talk. Why would the doorbell ring? Perhaps this was a sign that Jim was still here in spirit.

Reflecting on things Jim has told me, which remain very important to me. He said that "Your writing is a gift for the world," "You can work out all the demons," "I'm honored that I was able to help you. You trusted me, and that's huge, for any human being." The last thing he said to me was: "Bye-bye my friend." He died two weeks later, and I was very upset as he died on a day when we usually talked.

On the 4th of March I sent Jim this note: "Thank you for all your help. As I mentioned to you March 3rd 2022, and you agreed, that we had a connection and kinship. My love and task for the future are my memoirs. These help me with self-awareness, realization, and actualization. I guess it could be called 'memoir therapy and analysis.' So, good luck Jim with your Sunday zoom calls with your daughters. By the way, your laughter is healing. Glad you can zoom your humor to your family." Along with this message I sent Jim two poems, which I write below.
Alone

allows one to be
all one
Alone
with a
full moon

Chapter Ten

Physician, Heal Thyself

Toward the end of March on the 26th, I had an idea for a book, the *Tao of Analysis: Finding Meaning Through In-Depth Understanding and Connection*. On reflecting on this now I realize that if someone wanted to understand me and my philosophy, they could just read all the books that I've written. And of course, being a bit pro myself, it's a good idea for me to read all the stuff I've written as well – this, I believe, is spoken out of a healthy narcissism.

On Saturday May 7th I had a dream that I had gotten a new job as director of some organization, evaluating the role of suicidal ideation in a teen population. This is a huge problem in our society. Also, my goddaughter and her partner Ibi came to visit. We had a lovely time, and Lanara made a delicious homemade soup which was perfect. Ibi and Annahita visited again the next day and brought some rolls from a bakery. This was kind and thoughtful. They left for Portland because Ibi has a friend there.

After they left, I had an unusual thought, that the very next day, my mother would have been 108 – this was 15 years after her death in 2008.

On Wednesday, May 25th, I had a dream of Lanara, my lovely, smart, talented and creative wife. This dream was very important to me, as I will never forget all these aspects of her personality.

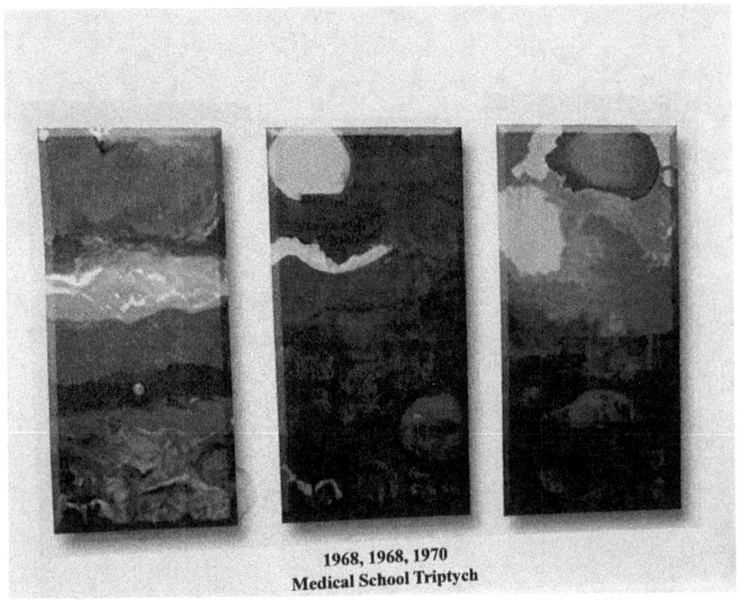
1968, 1968, 1970
Medical School Triptych

These were made as all art projects are: to promote one's mental health and psychic balance. To say the least, medical school was difficult, but rewarding. You can see that in these paintings, in a way. The bottom part is dark, but has green in it, for nature. The middle part in the two paintings on the right are red, which often mean danger. Going to medical school allowed me to have an experience with very ill and dying patients, which probably relates to my own despair and search for sunshine and blue skies. It's clear to me that the bright colors indicate that my soul was striving for wholeness.

I had seen an ad in the newspaper for these blank canvases. When I went to look at them, the person told me that they were beds for little children who were in preschool. I was struck by this fact because as children, we spontaneously draw and paint. So, what I was doing in an unconscious way was linking my struggles to that time in my life. These paintings today are in the private collection of Alex Weston, in Eugene, Oregon.

It was wonderful for Laura to have visited in May, and we know her life will be full, exciting, and complete.

I dreamt of Lanara, my lovely, smart, talented, and creative wife. In my dream Lanara represented herself and my anima, which is connected to "animated," which is linked to a man's creative process. Outside of my dreams, in the world, there is a lot of wind and rain. I am sad that my MS has numbed my left side, my arm and my leg. On May 29th I dreamt of an overweight fellow who wanted to date a woman, and asked for my help. I suggested that he lose weight, work out, and exercise.

I dreamt on May 30th that I was back at UC Berkeley with the Free Speech Movement (FSM). This was an exciting time, and I felt myself living again in a moment that had passed. I remember when Mario Savio (a Physics major) jumped up on top of a police car and said: "We have the right to speak our minds." At his call, we sat in the administration building and were inspired to bring the university to a grinding halt. I recall Joan Baez singing "We shall overcome." "It took a while, and all the students were rounded up and penned inside of a race track, a makeshift prison. Eventually everyone was released, but only after Pat Brown, the governor, was called in. This was the first mass act of civil disobedience on an American college campus in the 1960s and it led to the eventual end of the Vietnam War.

Being pre-med, I thought I had to get all my required finished: Chemistry, and so on. I went to the chemistry class one day and the professor had written across the board "Class Canceled. Go to Sproul Plaza in front of the Administration Building and support FSM." This was a movement of students and faculty. I thought this was how all universities operated. He said occupy Sproul Hall, and so we had a sit in there. Walking along the hallway came Joan Baez, a known activist and brilliant performer, singing "We shall overcome."

Rachel visited with my first granddaughter Ember on June 6th, 2022. I had trouble sleeping the night before out of anticipation, and my desire to live. I want to see Ember go to Harvard, or wherever she chooses to end up. I gave Rachel and Lia (her partner) a copy of my children's book *Kindergarten Symphony* for Ember, a book about learning the alphabet.

At this time in my life Alex Weston was helping me type. We were working on a poetry collection called *Opening Our Hearts*, which was published later that year. In this particular June the weather was cool and warm, not yet so hot as are my memories of Texas.

Afterword

Writing memoir is a type of self-analysis that is healing for the author. To end this volume I want to say a few words about my recent life: During 2023, I released five more books: *Night Owl Haiku: A Long-Distance Collaboration* with Robert Epstein, *Valor to Live: Beyond Despair, Synchronicity and Individuation: A Primer of Jung's Analytical Psychology* and my third memoir, *Finding Love and Life: Healing The Soul* and *Roses: Collection of Little Poems*. Now I want to share a little part of each book with you. If someone were to read these books, they would know all about me.

From *Night Owl Haiku*:

At the river's edge
waiting
to cross over

From *Valor to Live*:

Look in the mirror and realize that you are unique and actualize your personal myth. Analyze to death your false suicidal self, not your true self. Like and love your true self and remember – seek help and become all you can be. Take care of your body and soul.

Afterword

From *Synchronicity and Individuation:*

The ego means "I" or the self-identity (different from Self – this will be expanded on later). Often, the repressed aspect of one's identity is split off as are the defenses (as outlined in a lovely little book by Anna Freud[1]). Part of the nature of in-depth therapy is to bring that split part back to the person as part of their wholeness. Ego psychology, which is prominent in our institutions and training, just focuses on the ego, which is like the American philosophy of 'look out for number one.' If you are just focused on individuality & not familial, and socio-cultural life then you are cut off from a full life, which tragically is not that uncommon in the United States and the western world. Fortunately, Jung had the idea to place the ego consciousness secondary to the Self.

From *Finding Love and Life, Healing the Soul:*

After a few days of meaningful time with Laura in the historic city of Cusco,Peru we took a delightful single track train south and then a bus up to Machu Picchu. Most people don't know this, but there is a place to stay up at the site called Sanctuary Lodge, which I learned about from a Shirley MacLaine book that I had read. Machu Picchu is a magical place. Once the tourists left to head down, we had the incredible, sacred place all to ourselves. When we were walking around the site we turned a corner and there was a llama!

Llama
face to face
at Machu Picchu

Roses:
Full moon
mandala morphing
in my heart

---

1. Freud, Anna. *The Ego and the Mechanisms of Defense.* This book has been republished by Routledge.

61

Embracing the Sunset Years and Looking Ahead

This collection, *Roses*, is a special topic for me, because its title is what my surname means. "Night Owl Haiku" was written with fellow haiku poet, Robert Epstein. We collaborated by sharing haiku. It celebrates our both being night owls. The other books speak for themselves. And, they concern topics dear to my heart and soul. Plus, they called on my knowledge and experience of teaching Analytical Psychology, Psychiatry and Humanities in Medicine at Texas A&M University in College Station, Texas for 25 years [1986–2017]. Currently. I am an Affiliate Professor of Psychiatry at OHSU.

2023 was a year of the Rabbit, which might explain why I produced as much as I did.

New Year's Day was happy. On January 2nd we interviewed James Miller. Jr. for a caregiver position. We both liked him. He was 56 and had worked in a nursing home before. However, he wanted to do independent work with a family. So, we hired him. It was interesting that he was a trained architect, which speaks about his intelligence. He also loved football and was a coach at the local Willamette High School. An advantage of James being a caretaker happened to me when I almost fell on a tile floor. But James caught me, so I was okay.

This brings this volume to a close. I wish the readers a wonderful creative and full life. Remember that all creative work begins with a dream and then a lot of hard work. However, the end product is worth the struggle and all the time and energy that goes into the project.